SILENT MUSIC

and other verse

written and illustrated

by

JOHN NURSEY

All proceeds from the sale of this book will be donated to the work of Macmillan Cancer Relief whose services include the provision of the Macmillan Nurses.

OTHER BOOKS BY JOHN NURSEY:

'WEEK-END IN THE VILLAGE and other verse'

'RIGHT TO ROAM and other verse'

© John Nursey 2001

Published by J.R. Nursey, Forge Cottage, Flaxton, York YO60 7RW

Printed and bound by York Publishing Services Ltd

ISBN 0 9535193 2 5

The cover photograph is a riverside scene at Beccles in Suffolk

CONTENTS

PREFACE

The remarkable and unexpected success of its two predecessors has led to the appearance of this third small collection of verse. As with the two earlier books I make no apology for the subject matter or nature of the verse, which has been written purely for my own pleasure and amusement. Some of the poems are frivolous and light hearted, some more serious and nostalgic, being recollections of places, people or incidents long passed. Others are of passing observations on modern life.

The verse is again supplemented with pen and ink sketches. Few, I have to say, have any direct relevance to the individual poems. They are included merely in the hope that they will add to the book's general interest. Most represent locations featured in the novels of Thomas Hardy, for which I have great affection.

Forge Cottage   John Nursey
Flaxton

Lower Bockhampton School
(Under the Greenwood Tree)

Looking for a Miracle

I wonder if at any time
There's anybody who
Has gone from Malton into York
And not sat in a queue
Of traffic mounted up behind
A tractor, doing ten
Or fifteen steady miles per hour,
And slowing now and then;
Because if such a man exists
Somewhere throughout the land
I'd like to meet him face to face
And shake him by the hand.

1

The Piece of Paper

Tucked in a book for forty years
    The small loose sheet has lain,
And always when that book I read
    I see it there again.

In clear round hand upon the sheet
    In pencil there are set
The names of plants once given me
    In case I would forget.

'Campanula Isophylla'
    And 'Caryopteris'
('Prune to four eyes in early spring')
    With other notes to this.

The giver of these plants and notes,
    How clear I see him still,
Though long he's slept below the ground
    He nurtured with a will.

A former master at my school,
    Retired to cottage life;
We'd called soon after we were wed
    To see him and his wife.

He went, a young man, to the school,
    Was loved by everyone;
As Second Master he'd returned
    When World War Two was done.

He taught us how to keep the goal,
   And careful draughtsmanship;
And how to chisel joints in wood,
   With loving craftsmanship.

A kindly man of quiet taste
   With humour in his eyes,
And when he married late in life
   He took us by surprise.

'Free period', he'd wryly say,
   'I had that afternoon.
No books to mark, so we got wed.
   Seemed somehow opportune'.

Long dead his plants and he as well,
   But happy was that day
He welcomed us and we were young
   And chanced to be his way.

These hoarded papers tucked in books
   I clear out now and then;
But always at that sheet I pause,
   Then put it back again.

The Signboard Men

These days when I go somewhere new I always fear the worst;
I know some fool with painted signs has doubtless been there first.
'Keep to the path', 'Please mind your head', 'No adults on the swing',
'At your own risk', 'No entry here', – you know the sort of thing.

Across the Country men at desks sit working on some text,
And dreaming up a likely place to put a new sign next.
Get in your car, drive anywhere; you'll find since you went last
There'll be at least one added sign to read as you go past.

It's Highways men who lead the field as painted signboard breeders
But when it comes to silliness they are not quite the leaders;
Environmental Agency – they play the stronger hand.
(The proper word's 'Environment' but that would not have scanned).

Whichever way you say it though, it's meaningless and crass,
A title doubtless dreamt up by some bureaucratic ass.
Although best known for causing floods, the Agency outshines
All others in the lunacy with which it puts up signs.

Near us a brook six inches deep and barely three feet wide
Now has 'Deep Water' warning signs set all along its side;
And on these yellow painted signs, in case the words you miss,
There is a diagram to show just what deep water is.

If it were not so ludicrous you'd have to stop and smile.
They're set three hundred yards apart – about six to the mile.
No matter how remote the spot their men have been there too,
And put up signs to tell you all the things you must not do.

I know a little river bridge where once the railway ran
But now it's got great yellow signs at each end of the span.
'No Diving', these, with diagrams to make them understood;
Though no-one ever has dived in, and no-one ever would.

If you should walk along our brook the first thing that you'll see
Are ten assorted warning signs, these mostly M.O.D.
'Troops Training' (large), 'Troops Training' (small), a red flag on a pole,
'No Vehicles', 'Keep Access Clear', and 'Keys at Range Control'.

'Troops Training' is their favourite sign and set in roadside grass
In half a mile along the road there's thirteen that you'll pass.
This sign, it baffles me a bit. Who wants to be aware
That troops are training? Or indeed, does anybody care?

Disclaimers are the latest fad put up for us to read,
Denying liability with yards and yards of screed.
'The Council can accept no blame' – this point they strongly make,
And strangely, always close to where your parking fee they take.

Out on a moor remote and wild, where often I go back
There is upon a ladder stile a County Council plaque.
It smugly says the stile is theirs; and oh dear, how perverse,
'A Countryside Initiative', which makes it even worse.

No doubt at heart these bureaucrats are really just like us,
With wives and cars and mortgages, and sometimes swear and cuss.
I'm sure these men with painted signs don't mean to give offence,
It's just that, sadly, what they lack is any common sense.

Puddletown
(Far from the Madding Crowd)

Lines written when idling through a book of Frank Sutcliffe's photographs

I idly turn in this old book
Each haunting sepia printed page,
And at another world I look
Of distant harsh but tranquil age.

These photographs of long ago,
All centred on this seaside place,
Reveal a life we'll never know
Contained within each captured face.

And somehow I am backwards drawn
In to that age, where every scene
Suggests to me some hardship borne
Or joys and fears there might have been.

Here ragged urchins play and laugh;
Here cart with horse that slowly plods;
Top hatted railway station staff;
Here chimney sweep with brush and rods.

Across the harbour in full sail
Here moves a pair of Whitby yawls;
Here women at the harbour rail;
Here ancient dames with crocheted shawls.

What scenes of drama are set here
That hauntingly these pages show,
Though crude the camera, plates, and gear
That captured them so long ago.

These fisher girls along the Quay –
Did they perhaps keep watch and pray
On nights when wildly raged the sea
For loved ones safe return next day?

These boys around a boat at play
In eighteen eighty six; what then
The fate of all these lads, when they
Had grown to working Whitby men?

This lifeboatman what tales might tell
Of shipwrecks, gallant deeds he knew;
Who, when one tragedy befell,
Was sole survivor of his crew.

Hard was their life and never free,
Yet still within each homely face
That from the page looks out to me
A quiet contentment there I trace.

A hundred years have now gone by,
And lanes and yards and homes and Quay
Now modern faces occupy;
But few show joy it seems to me.

Now we are free, no more the threat
Of workhouse, poverty, or pain,
And comfortable our life; and yet
Man's heart in joy shows little gain.

The Friary Mill, Dorchester
(The Mayor of Casterbridge)

The City Walls, York

The Treasurer's Report

When I attend the AGM,
  So we can keep it short
I always hope nobody's read
  The Treasurer's Report.

But, sure as fate, some bright spark has,
  And always wonders why
The 'Postage' costs for this past year
  Seem really rather high.

And what does 'Sundry Charges' mean?
  Should we more detail keep?
Thank God, before this fool has done
  I'm usually asleep.

The Expedition

Here where the lane to westward veers
Below a cloudless Norfolk sky,
I see again across the years
A youthful pair go cycling by.

Myself when young, and she beside,
One carefree early August day,
When down this country lane we'd ride
And harvest fields about us lay.

How fast we glided down the hill
Beyond that clump of roadside trees!
Then stirred the air with speeding thrill,
Her long skirt flowing in the breeze.

We'd used a pin to mark a dot
Upon the map, we cared not where;
Then cycled out to find that spot
And picnic in the summer air.

Far from the road we had to search,
And wheel our bicycles beyond
An isolated little church
Down by some alders and a pond.

We picnicked in the long marsh grass
With skylarks singing high above,
And let the sultry hours pass,
So happy there and so in love.

And nothing stirred in all that time
Of languid calm and summer drowse,
Save one train on a far off line
And idle drift of grazing cows.

The parsley down the roadside verge
Smells just as sweetly now as then,
And somehow past and present merge
And I am just a lad again.

But then the mists of time roll clear,
And I'm aware with sudden start
Of one old man just lingering here,
Time worn, and with an empty heart.

For she who rode will ride no more
About these winding Norfolk lanes,
Or picnic as she did before,
And idly watch the distant trains.

And what became of that young lad
Who cycled down this lane so free?
What happened to the dreams he had
That he became someone like me?

But O what joy the memories hold
Of that far day and more beside;
A lasting joy that grows not cold
As slowly ebbs my falling tide.

Old Books

What a feast is here to regale myself,
I ponder, each time that my books I view,
As I trace my finger along the shelf
And lovingly scan the covers anew.

In a rambling fashion for row on row
Each book resides in its ordered place;
A world into which I can delve and go,
Re-visit old scenes or a well loved face.

Here Hornblower battles with French man-of-war;
Here Tess is at Trantbridge in D'Urberville's gig;
Here Hannay is striding high up on the moor.
At Blandings Lord Emsworth communes with his pig;

Here nestles a book of the great Bard's plays;
What riches are there that never grow dim!
With many old friends since my schoolboy days,
Falstaff and Pistol and Bardolph and Nym.

I reach for a book in some idle hour
And randomly open at any odd page,
Feel drawn to the past as the lines I scour
On the musty leaf now yellowed with age.

Whose hands, I wonder, first handled this book
When printed in nineteen hundred and ten?
And how many readers have chanced to look
On this page in the numerous years since then?

Were they all, I wonder, the same as I,
Joyful or sad as the story decreed?
And were they drawn too, as the scenes went by,
In a personal way to each thought or deed?

Silently now through each generation
Hand upon hand in my dreaming I see
Turning the page with due veneration,
Moved by the story the way it moves me.

All round me now as I doze by the fire
Lurks a world of Hardy and Watson and Holmes,
Three Men in Boat, and the Mellstock choir,
And Jolyon Forsyte, and Irene and Soames.

Without friends like these how cheerless our path;
No poor crippled Smike to give us all hope;
No laughter with Wodehouse, or lewd Wife of Bath,
Or Wilkins Micawber, or Reverend Slope.

A house without books – how drear that must be,
A place with no soul; no book now and then
To handle and hold, and know you are free
To delve and enjoy it again and again.

Mrs Robinson

Good Morning, Mrs Robinson,
    Off to the Hunt, I see,
To join your demonstrating friends
    And help the fox get free.

Although you little comprehend
    The thing you wish to ban
I quite agree at times like these
    One must do what one can.

To follow hounds that chase and kill,
    That must be bad enough;
Enjoying it just makes it worse,
    So go and do your stuff.

But hang on, Mrs Robinson,
    Please tell me this, I pray,
How many mice and little birds
    Has your cat killed today?

And when you put slug pellets down
    Or poison for the rat
How ghastly is the lingering death?
    Please, could you tell me that?

But surely you don't keep a cat
    And poison don't permit,
I do hope, Mrs Robinson,
    You're not a hypocrite.

And may I just say one more thing
  Before you start your car?
Your banner wording's very droll
  But 'bastards' has one 'r'.

Tincleton
(The Return of the Native)

15

Hardy's Birthplace, Higher Bockhampton
(Under the Greenwood Tree)

The Music of Youth

Through London streets and lanes each day
By foot at work I would arrive
From where I lodged five miles away;
And by such means I did contrive
To save the fares that I would pay
From Clapham on a forty five.

A week of toiling on my feet
And I had then the wherewithal
To visit in the cheapest seat
A concert at the South Bank hall,
And there my joy would be complete
As Bach and Brahms did me enthral.

Behind the orchestra my pew,
From where conductors' forms I'd face;
See Barbarolli's hair askew,
Watch Boult's serene and stately grace,
While orchestras with joy anew
Transformed me to some heavenly place.

No gramophone, no radio,
Just hard earned concerts now and then;
And never did I ever know
When Delius I'd hear again,
Or Beethoven that I loved so,
Or Elgar, Brahms or Mendelssohn.

Now in my house I sit at ease,
And turn a switch with idle touch
To hear whatever works I please;
Near perfect sound – but is it such
A sound as precious as were these
Long distant strains that thrilled so much?

The Spirit of Christmas Present

From mid November 'Jingle Bells'
In supermarket wails
To get us in the festive mood
And boost their Christmas sales.
And now the day is drawing near
Heaped high upon the trolley
Are cans of beer and cakes and crisps
And imitation holly.

Within this blur of rush and din
A face I seem to see –
A little starving desert boy
Who's looking straight at me.
Bewilderment upon his face,
And both his parents dead,
He sits forlornly in the sand
As flies crawl on his head.

Emaciated, bag of bones,
With sunken hollow cheek;
Though nothing's said we know that he'll
Be dead within the week.
He touched our conscience for a while
But news moves quickly on,
And though the starving boy remains
The TV crews have gone.

Unendingly and mounted high
The bulging trolleys come;
A pop star churns out 'Silent Night',
The tills at check-outs hum.
Then homeward with a loaded car
To gorge the hours away
In front of mindless TV shows
Through all of Christmas Day.

The vacant eyes look on at me,
So much they seem to say;
They hold me there, though hard I try
To turn my head away.
And as they look they seem to ask
'Could it be really so,
It was for this that Christ was born
In stable long ago?'

Bere Heath
(The Return of the Native)

19

Ask the Ghosts

Ask the ghosts who loiter there
Along that lonely western shore,
If thirty years ago and more
They do recall the loving pair.

A pair who sauntered hand in hand
By shoreline when the tide was out,
No other living soul about
And all was sea and sky and sand.

So happy in the warm sea air,
So deep in love and young and free,
Each thought no time there'd ever be
When the hand they held would not be there.

Of that pair now one dreaming, sees
A figure walking as before
Along that fond remembered shore,
Of distant joy and languid ease.

But now no more the sky is blue,
No more there clasps the loving hand,
And now the footprints in the sand
Show one by one, not two by two.

O ask the ghosts why love is cruel,
And such a ruthless course to choose,
So much to win; so much to lose
When snatched away like priceless jewel.

A Norfolk Wherry

The Gawpers

Our rowing boat nosed through the reeds
  Below the bankside trees,
Where we could sit and eat our lunch
  In shelter from the breeze.

Then presently around a bend
  A wherry came in view;
Adapted as a pleasure boat,
  With passengers and crew.

The seats, all facing to the front,
　　Across the deck were spread,
With thirty passengers or more,
　　All staring straight ahead.

The great red sail, stirred by the breeze,
　　In silence slowly neared,
Until it drew abreast of us
　　And we to them appeared.

Then thirty heads all turned as one,
　　In snooping silent stare;
And gawped at us, intent to see
　　What we were doing there.

I thought of things I'd like to shout;
　　'These sandwiches are meat';
And many other apt remarks
　　It's best I don't repeat.

Then one by one their heads turned back
　　To face the front anew;
But some of them gawped on until
　　We'd faded from their view.

Then later on as we rowed back,
　　What joy, when there we found
The wherry, having missed a bend,
　　Had firmly run aground.

Half up upon the bank it sat,
　　Put there by nature's powers,
Marooned, and – how we rubbed our hands –
　　It would be there for hours.

The gawpers turned to watch us pass,
　　But now with sombre stare;
We gave them all a beaming smile
　　And left them sitting there.

Good manners just prevented me;
　　Though tempted sore was I
To put two fingers up at them
　　As we rowed freely by.

Then back in town, as we tied up,
　　Although it was a sin
We felt a sense of added joy
　　For rain had now set in.

Stinsford Church
(Under the Greenwood Tree)

23

Lot 261

Lot two-six-one at Beccles Sale
'A box of miscellaneous books,'
On view where oddments all prevail
And no prospective dealer looks.

Adventure story books for boys
With heroes, battles, friend, and foe,
Enthralling surely, with great joys,
Some boy a hundred years ago.

Before the Auctioneers proceed
I pause amidst the Saleroom din,
Take up a book and casually read
Inscriptions written there within.

A school prize this in nineteen one,
'Dog Crusoe', by R. Ballantyne.
'Good conduct and for good work done.'
Presented to a Frederick Dyne.

A bright young lad Fred must have been,
More prizes here the boy had won;
'Cambries Chief Tain' by Everett Green,
And poetry by Tennyson.

And here 'The Hero of the Hills'
A story by G. Weldo Browne –
Another book of boyhood thrills,
With pages worn and corners down.

Ah! Nineteen seven, his school days done;
Now at the Postal Telegraph
This 'David Copperfield' he'd won
As messenger on their behalf.

What did life hold for young Fred Dyne?
Was he, perhaps, a few years on
In trenches fighting in the line,
And died at Ypres or Amiens?

Or did he live to prove himself
On Norfolk farm with Norfolk wife,
His prize books set along some shelf
As he advanced to later life?

These books – so old, so proudly won
By him with schoolboy grin and locks –
All dumped; his time, and theirs, now done,
Discarded in a cardboard box.

And when the selling has begun
'Tis likely anybody who
Might want to have Lot two-six-one
Will spend but just a pound or two.

Evershed
(Tess of the D'Ubervilles)

The Telegram

Lengthening days of early spring,
Blackbirds' nests and mad March hares;
Little sign that fate might bring
News to take us unawares.

Young, my mother, fair and shy,
Dad a soldier in the war,
Though at seven 'twas true that I
Little knew what war was for.

Breakfast time as we sat down
Came a knock of heavy swing,
Rose my mother with a frown
Fearful what the knock might bring.

Words I heard – my mother's name –
'No reply' – the front door slam;
Ashen faced my mother came,
In her hand the telegram.

Mother weeping in her chair,
Nothing stirring; nothing said;
Furtively while standing there
I took up the sheet and read.

Phrases then I vaguely caught,
'To inform' and 'with regret'
'Killed in Action' – words that brought
Grief I never would forget.

Still I see the flickering grate;
Her sad face as tear-drops rolled;
Mantle clock then showing eight;
Untouched breakfasts long since cold.

Trudging then down Willow Lane,
White with hedges blossom clad,
With the news and coming pain
For his waiting mum and dad.

The Red House, near Wantage
(Jude the Obscure)

High Upon the Snow Clad Moor

High upon the snow clad moor
Crisp's the air and clear and bright,
Ivelet in the valley floor
Far below lies wrapped in white.

Nothing stirs in all the dale,
Save at one far distant spot
Smoke drifts up in rising trail
From a farmhouse chimney pot.

Glistening white the moor is spread
In the sunlit morning glow,
Silent, save for crunching tread
Of my footsteps in the snow.

By my path a dead sheep lies,
Far from flock and homely fold,
Stark and still with staring eyes,
Frozen hard but feels no cold.

Soon will be, while lying there,
Torn apart by fox and crow;
Soon will both those eyes that stare
Only empty sockets show.

Flown, its soul - to who knows where?
Left the body where it lay
Lifeless in the moorland air,
Food for fox and bird of prey.

When the summer breezes lull
Round this wild and lonely place
Scattered bones and empty skull
Will remain its only trace.

What a transitory thing
Is all life upon the earth!
Life to which we vainly cling,
Filling days to little worth.

Few the valued things I've done
Or will do before I die,
When my earthly course is run
And I too will rotting lie.

Brief is life, so I must go
Striding out and all cares ban,
See the beauty of the snow
On the moorlands while I can.

The Nouveau Rustique

He's something in the City and he's worth a bob or two
And thought a Suffolk country patch was something he'd pursue,
Where he could be a countryman and lead a country life
When he came down at each week-end (with someone else's wife).

He bought old Charlie Farrow's place when Charlie passed away,
A bit run down but with great scope for someone who could pay.
Within six months it was transformed, and when the work was done
The country cottage had become all very Islington.

All gone the rambling hawthorn hedge with dog rose wild and thick
And in its place a wrought iron fence on inappropriate brick.
The lawns are trim and manicured with neatly gravelled drive,
And ornaments, and garden lights to bring it all alive.

The little lane down by his house where airguns once we'd fire
With subtlety and by degrees he's working to acquire.
His four wheel drive obstructs the path, his wolfhound lounges there;
It bares its teeth as you approach – you pass it if you dare.

With cowslip, may, and willow-herb this leafy track was strewn
But now his strimmer blasts away each Sunday afternoon.
Suburban now it starts to look, all trimly cut and lined,
Already with his garden ground you'd think it was combined.

And in the 'Plough' on Friday nights when he arrives from town
He dominates the public bar with friends that he's brought down;
Their conversation loud and brash with many knowing winks,
And big cigars, and mobile phones, as they knock back the drinks.

On Saturdays it's barbecues with music turned up high,
Bad luck for those in Northgate Lane whose houses are nearby.
The smell and noise pervades the street till late on in the night
As louder grows the *bonhomie* the more his pals get tight.

No one more keen to save the shop and stop it closing down,
Though when he comes his week-end food comes with him from the town.
Occasionally he does call in when passing by that way,
But just to buy a postage stamp and pass the time of day.

It's clear to all he's keen to use his managerial skills
To bring the village up to date and remedy our ills.
He's agitating hard to get street lights and yellow lines,
And roadside kerbs, and tourist maps, and far more traffic signs.

He sees himself as gentry here, so likes to condescend
To now and then drive down to church and services attend.
It makes him part of village life and sort of one of us,
And though he does not know the man he calls our vicar 'Russ'.

Thank God on Monday he'll be gone and back in EC2,
Then empty will his smart house stand until the week is through;
'NO CALLERS' showing on a sign and padlocks on the gates,
Till back he comes on Friday night with all his ghastly mates.

Yet in this little Suffolk church, among the elms and yews,
You realise that time's moved on as you glance round the pews;
My brother at the organ, Fred Bly, and Mrs Plym,
And both the Shaws, but all the rest are townies just like him.

Silent Music

The river at the break of day
Far from the haunts of men,
Where mists of early autumn lay
Across the Norfolk fen.

And willows at the water's edge
Stand motionless and tall,
With morning dew upon the sedge
Where alders lean and sprawl.

About this early morning place
Of neither stir nor sound
Within the stillness there I trace
Some presence all around.

How little do we comprehend
The power that silence holds,
That somehow makes our souls ascend
As round us it enfolds.

In great cathedral high and vast,
Or church down country lane,
Some holy stillness there is cast
We feel but can't explain.

Among the hills new strength we draw
From heath and mountain air,
And in the silence of the moor
We feel God's presence there.

What lifts our soul with such strange thrill
When silence is around,
When all the world is calm and still
And solitude is found?

Great music is a lovely thing,
And larks and nightingales,
But only can their joy they bring
When silence too, prevails.

The willows whispering in the breeze,
A bumble bee in flight;
The drip of rain from woodland trees,
A barn owl in the night.

Earth's differing music rapture brings,
Yet this for sure I know –
For all the beauty of these things
'Tis silence makes it so.

The Red Lion, Winfrith
(The Return of the Native)

The Soldiers' Return

Round the bend by Ingate crossing
Steamed the slowing London train;
Back from war to town and farmstead
Beccles lads came home again.

Down they stepped to station platform
Breathing homely Suffolk air,
To the arms and friendly faces
Of their loved ones waiting there.

Safe returned to wives and sweethearts,
Full of laughter, homeward bound
To their houses in the borough
And the villages around.

The Guard's flag waved; the train pulled out;
Soon the platform silence wrought,
The train its happy discharge made,
But my dad it had not brought.

Alone she sat by the fireside
My mum with her aching loss,
And thought of a grave in the desert,
And the name on its makeshift cross.

Manners Maketh Man

When you are driving in your car
Along a country lane
And meet a rider on a horse
It happens in the main
That as you slow right down for them,
When they are passing you,
While men will always raise a hand
Young women seldom do.

Sometimes you get, as you crawl by,
A condescending stare,
But mostly they look straight ahead
Their nose stuck in the air.
'You wait, my girl,' I always think,
'Next time I'm passing you
I'll put my foot down; serve you right.'
But then I never do.

These days they want to be like men;
Wear trousers, play men's games
Like cricket, football, rugby; and
Be called by Christian names.
'Equality in everything,'
Is their eternal cry;
So why is it when on a horse
Good manners don't apply?

The Mist on the Moor

A morning mist hung on the moor
When I set out today,
Up by the Chapel through the wood
Along the hillside way,
Where all was bleak and grey.

Now passed a crumbling ruined barn
And bridge across the beck
Along the lonely moorland path
Through thickening mist I trek,
And frosts the ways bedeck.

Small scattered pools lie frozen hard
About the peaty ground,
While now and then a startled grouse
From in the heather round
Creates the only sound.

Here, where the mist encircles me,
I feel about me then
From near two hundred years ago
Come lingering again
The ghosts of mining men.

A watery sun breaks through the mist
High up by Moor House Gill,
Where solitude and silence hangs
Upon the winter hill,
And all the world is still.

And in that wild and silent place
I sense, as I stride there,
How distant and how trivial
As if by answered prayer
Grows all my worldly care.

The Faringdon Ruin
(The Trumpet Major)

The River Stour

Ryedale

Though far from Ryedale's homely soil
    Where distant duties draw
My heart lies in the heather still,
    High up on Wheeldale Moor.

And O that I was striding now
    Across the moorland hills,
Or down on Farndale's winding paths
    Among the daffodils.

In Castle Howard gardens now,
    Along the great Lime Walk
The wood anemones will show
    A carpet white as chalk.

When London streets burn in the sun
   And stale's the air and dry
I wonder if the meadowsweet
   Is out along the Rye;

And if Dick Green has started yet
   On bringing in the hay;
And what the fatstock heifers made
   At Malton sales today.

When winter slush is all around
   And London glooms prevail
I wonder if the wolds are white
   With snow, at Thixendale;

And if the winter sun shines down
   On Rievaulx in the snow;
And if they sledge at Terrington,
   Where we boys used to go.

Ah Ryedale! With your lovely hills
   And crisp clear moorland air,
Oh how I hold you in my heart
   And wish that I was there.

Lower Bockhampton Bridge
(Under the Greenwood Tree)

False Hopes

When you drop toast it is well known
    That when it hits the floor
It lands with buttered side face down,
    Acknowledged as sod's law.

Today my toast went to the floor
    (I'd knocked it with my cup),
But when I looked, to my surprise
    The buttered side was up.

The first time ever, this, for me,
    And straightway I was struck
With wondering if from now on
    In life I'd have more luck.

I told this to a friend today,
    'My luck has changed,' I cried.
'Oh no,' he said, 'it merely means
    You buttered the wrong side.

Life's Mysteries

So many things there are in life
    That really puzzle me,
And no-one has an answer to
    As far as I can see.

When I am late and in a queue
    And time is pressing hard,
Why is it that the man in front
    Can't find his Credit Card?

When at some eating place I call
    To have a cup of tea
Why does some smoker always come
    And sit right near to me?

And why does all the wafting smoke
    Come heading straight my way
When he goes out and leaves his fag
    Half smoked upon the tray?

Why is it when I buy a shirt
    And one has been agreed,
They've got that shirt in every size
    Except the size I need?

And people who tow caravans,
    (A carefree life is theirs),
Why is it in the summer months
    They always drive in pairs?

And when they start out on their way
    Do they set off in twos?
Or do they lurk in some lay-by,
    Their travelling mate to choose?

And why do characters in films
    When they are drinking tea
Drink out of empty cups or mugs?
    That's odd, you must agree.

Why do they never lock their cars,
    In streets or market place?
And how is it, I'd like to know,
    There's always parking space?

And sportsmen when they're interviewed,
    Especially the young,
Why is that the English ones
    Can't speak their native tongue?

Why, when on open space I park,
    Do I return to see
The only other car that's come
    Is parked two feet from me?

Why is it when I'm in the shower
    That glazing salesmen call?
And men on trains with mobile phones,
    Why were they born at all?

Such things as these and more besides
    No matter how I try
I never can quite fathom out
    Or know the reason why.

When I am Gone

When I am gone will any say
"A useful life he led;
He left the world a better place,
We're sorry that he's dead."?
Or will men tell a different tale?
"He was aloof and shy;
We never quite knew who he was
And never wondered why.

The ancient towers and City walls
That stretch for mile on mile
He kept in place and good repair
With engineering guile.
He loved the walls and monuments,
He felt them as his own,
He seemed to know each secret place
And nearly every stone.

But Engineers they come and go
Who work on tower and wall;
Their names, like his and those before,
Are soon beyond recall.
The memory of what he did,
And labours that he made,
Already now is history
And dead, I am afraid.

For who will say, as they sit down
In buildings far and near,
'This structural frame he did design;
Each stanchion, beam, and pier'?
'Tis sad, but no-one ever thinks
About the person, whose
Designs and calculations made
Their building safe to use.

He loved the place where he did live;
But with a change of heart,
In village life in later years
He took but little part.
In truth we did not know him well,
He seemed to amble on,
Was not a man you took to much,
We hardly know he's gone."

It little serves to think upon
The legacy we'll leave,
What men might say for good or ill
Of all we did achieve.
For sure it is the time will come,
As quickly come it must,
That those who judge us when we've gone
Will all themselves be dust.

Water Tower, York City Defences

The Hip Operation

My premiums are all paid up; a brand new hip for me.
Insurance is a wondrous thing, and I'm with PPP.
We've got off to a dodgy start – an omen, I suspect,
They call me Mr. Nursery, which isn't quite correct.

Already I have got cold feet from what they're asking me;
'What other things are wrong with you? And are you C of E?'
But worst of all, it seems to me, as forms they now fill in,
Is that they mainly want to know who is my next of kin.

'Your surgeon's very nice,' they say. 'His name is Mr. Spear.'
Spear? What a terrifying name; that's tripled now my fear.
Did he come here from Zanzibar? I start to sweat and cough,
And wonder if it's too late now to call the whole thing off.

'You may find that your bowels won't work, it happens now and then.
It might require an enema to help things move again.
And sometimes it's a catheter, we'll have to wait and see.'
O God, this nightmare's getting worse. Is there no hope for me?

With mounting dread the hours drag on, but now the time is near
That I must go and have my hip lanced out by Mr. Spear.
It's not the hip that worries me, it's if my bowel fails
And they give me an enema with all that that entails.

I lie here in my theatre gown, my mind grows dim and blunt,
I'm not sure if this gown's on right, or if it's back to front.
Now here they come – they're wheeling me, with many a jolt and jerk
- A face peers down – they prick my arm – O please God let it work.

Now everything's turned out all right, I'm happy to report,
And when the fearsome nurse comes round I'll joyfully retort
To her vociferous demand, relating to the lav,
'And have we moved our bowels today?' O yes nurse, yes we have.

I like the dark haired Sister best, she lets me go for walks;
And sometimes sits beside my bed and laughs and jokes and talks.
The little fair haired one's quite nice with tempting grey blue eyes,
But she's too keen to keep me in with endless exercise.

Some foreign doctor's reading now the notes hooked on my bed.
But will he know, when he has done, exactly what he's read?
Please may his English be all right; O please God, let it, please;
You never can be certain with these chaps from overseas.

'You're walking well with just one stick, that is a splendid sign'
(But – just in case – I tell him that my bowels are doing fine).
'The room is booked ten days for this, so you can see it through.
But if you like you can go home; I'll leave it up to you.'

The premiums, they cost a bomb; too much for what I earn.
For years I've strived to keep them up, with little in return.
I've rather got to like this place, I'll stay another day,
And lounge, and I'll be waited on. And PPP will pay.

The Unimpressed Reader

Thank God this is the final page,
At last the book is done;
It beggars all belief to think
He wrote this stuff for fun.

The Keeper's Cottage, Yellowham Wood
(Under the Greenwood Tree)